DAD, UNSOLICITED

OBSERVATIONS ON LIFE

BY GUY RAYMAKER

FIRST EDITION

Cover illustration by Luke Raymaker

ISBN 979-8-9920999-0-4 (paperback)

ISBN 979-8-9920999-1-1 (e-book)

For my wonderful wife, Helen, and children: Abigail, Tim and Luke

A man could not ask for more

Contents

Introduction - To My Children

"The unexamined life is not worth living" - Socrates

Someone I once worked with early in my career came from humble roots (his father had been a bus driver) but achieved great success and wealth in business. His children had been raised in affluence and he once commented to me that it was too bad that his children had not been around to see how hard he and his wife struggled earlier in his career to achieve their financial success. He lived in a very beautiful house in one of the most expensive residential areas of San Francisco, but very few would have guessed that the Spanish tile that covered their backyard patio had been laid by hand by his wife and himself.

Similarly, the person I am today bears little resemblance to the person I started out to be. As a child I was smart, but not athletic. Our family moved a lot, so I was often being uprooted and faced with being "the new kid." This resulted in anxiety and low self-esteem. While I did well academically, I did not feel I had much to offer my peers and was sometimes bullied. I tended to dwell on my interactions with others and my place in the world, realizing that I did not fit in with my peers. I often felt isolated, especially in junior high and high school. It was around this time that I discovered Star Trek reruns on TV and came to identify with the alien, Mr. Spock. He successfully repressed his emotions, partly to cope with his lack of acceptance as either fully human or fully Vulcan. His character offered me some pathway as to how I could deal with my own feelings of isolation.

It was only through the kindness shown to me in high school by the girl who would one day become my wife and your mother that I finally began to feel worthy of the attention and love of others. The taunting I endured as a child would eventually give me the gift of caring less about the opinions of others. Still, I didn't feel like I exuded confidence. But one day, in my first year of working after college, my supervisor said, "not even a steamroller could run over you!" and I slowly began to realize that the way I was perceived by others was not consistent with the shy, insecure kid I still saw in myself.

This idea, that how we perceive ourselves and our own actions is often at odds with how others see us, has fascinated me my whole life. I continued to analyze (over-analyze?) the way people behave with each other, in some quixotic effort to better predict how people would react. I still find myself pointlessly reconsidering what I said in some interaction that might have occurred decades ago. My roommate in college used to say, "You think too much!", even though he would eventually earn his Phd from Stanford, so who was doing a lot of thinking?

I will turn 60 years old this year. In my career I have had to delve into the motivations of others, especially when they are stressed, in order to provide the best advice. I have continued to research human behavior and try to catalog in my own mind the various characters I have encountered and to understand their motivations. I am also aware of how much I have changed over this time. Even core beliefs, as simple as right and wrong, have shifted with more understanding.

I am also aware that as I get older, my thinking may not evolve as much as degrade with the advancement of age. I cannot help but consider at this stage of life that I have many more sunrises behind me than in front. Therefore, I have had in my mind for some time the idea of writing down some of my perspectives on life and living - both its joys and challenges. I also wish to capture for you what little wisdom I may have accumulated over my years. It doesn't mean that any of my ideas are correct, or if once correct, will withstand the continued evolving values of our society.

Humans are in a unique position to both actively consider their own lives and to record their thoughts beyond their own lifetime. Of course, not everyone does this. In fact, few do. Most people live and die without recording their perspectives or their understanding of their own lives. I saw my father evolve in his own thinking over time, only to have all his experience lost when he died suddenly. So, this is some small attempt to capture for you some of what I have observed and learned, while I still can. I hope you find it interesting.

Guy Raymaker, September 2024

The Role of Feelings

"In everything one thing is impossible: rationality"
- Friedrich Nietzsche

During my professional career, I became very interested in the process by which people make decisions. My job at the end of my career consisted of advising people amid difficult professional situations. In doing this, I was constantly amazed at the inability of intelligent people to view their own situation objectively. Their proximity to the events (and their fear of the impact upon themselves of a negative outcome), made it virtually impossible for them to make the kinds of observations and decisions that they were perfectly capable of making when the situation did not impact them so directly. In the hope of becoming a better advisor to them, I read extensively on the process of decision-making in order to better understand this phenomenon. In the process of doing this, I came to realize that, not only did people find it difficult to be objective in professional matters, but also in a host of personal decisions. People tend to be vulnerable to self-delusion and wildly overestimate the likelihood of a good (for confident people) or bad (for insecure people) outcome. Also, I came to realize that people generally have evolved to accurately evaluate short-

5

term risks to themselves (e.g., imminent danger), but are very poor at evaluating long-term risks (e.g., smoking). This makes sense in that accurate short-term risk evaluation is likely to have been favored by evolution, as you won't be able to realize any long-term risk skills if you get eaten by a lion in the short-term.

In a similar way, I believe that people are also un-skilled at evaluating what will make them happy. Evolution favors behaviors that will ensure the survival of the species; both the individual's survival (at least long enough to repro-duce) and the survival of the species as a whole. For most of mankind's existence, mere survival occupied all our thoughts and energy. Whether or not we are "happy" is irrelevant to evolution. As a result, people tend to misjudge the degree to which the achievement of their desires will make them happy. This is because their desires are a result of evolution's priorities (promulgation of the subject's genes), not the priorities of the subject themselves (i.e., hap-piness). For example, a man may desire many different sex-ual partners as this will maximize the promulgation of his genes, but such a lifestyle is less likely to result in the kinds of enduring and committed relationships that are most as-sociated with happiness.

The human brain was not created from a blank sheet of paper. Rather, it evolved from more primitive forms of life. So, our brains are built in layers, from the brain stem, which regulates autonomic functions (e.g., breathing) to the limbic system, which processes emotions. However, these emotions are processed in a basic way. For example, many people have heard of the "fight or flight" reflex when the emotion of fear is encountered. Animals process emotions in this way, which is useful for their survival, which is the whole point of evolution. However, mammals have additional structures, like the prefrontal cortex, which allows for higher level processing of emotions. Human brains have more of their brains dedicated to these brain functions than other animals. This allows us, should we choose, to reinterpret sensory and emotional input beyond the way in which our fellow mammals do. In other words, to rise above our programming and make decisions that are in our long-term interests, instead of just reacting to immediate stimuli. This is why your dog will never resist a treat in front of it, while we may decide that we aren't really hungry, and it would be better for our health to pass on dessert.

However, making choices which go against our basic programming requires extra effort and time, and we cannot afford to spend this effort and time on the millions of minor decisions we make each day. For example, we respond subconsciously to danger, because that is faster and thus increases survivability. So, to some degree, the differences between people consist of how much effort they expend on making conscious decisions vs. just letting their unconscious do almost all the work. I am sure we know people who seem to thoughtlessly move through their lives reacting to whichever situation they find themselves in, then being perplexed if things don't go their way. I believe that, since humans are capable (within limits, see below) of rising above their baseline reactions to stimuli, we have almost a moral imperative to do so; to do what is best for society (and ourselves) rather than simply reacting impulsively.

Despite the above admonition, there has been recent research that reveals even the existence of the "rational self" is a bit of a self-delusion. Our brain consists of different circuits evolved to process different stimuli, and our sense of one "rational self" that controls everything is a construct. The Interpreter Module of our brain coordinates and interprets all the noise from these various circuits and allows us to make sense of all the competing pieces of information to which we are constantly exposed. We make decisions at a subconscious level all the time, but this Interpreter Module of our brain works backwards to rationalize these subconscious decisions, as if we made them consciously, giving us more of a sense of control than we actually have. It is a complicated but fascinating topic, detailed in the book Who's in Charge by Dr. Michael Gazzaniga.

The conclusion of all these observations is that I believe a person should be very skeptical of their "feelings" when making decisions and, to the extent possible, override their feelings with unbiased, rational decision making to the extent possible. However, this is very difficult to achieve in practice. It is a lifelong pursuit, but worth the extra effort, because it can ultimately allow us to achieve the humanity and happiness each of us is capable of.

Success and Failure

"Never let success get to your head; never let failure get to your heart" - Anonymous

Most people, when they are young, dream of success. However, what "success" means is very different, not only to different people, but to the same people at different points in their lives. Younger people often dream of financial success and popularity (i.e., "rich and famous"). As people go through school, they may strive towards academic or athletic success, followed by dreams of career success as they embark on their work life. My own plans upon graduation consisted solely of having enough money to live on my own; to complete two years of public accounting to qualify for my CPA and then maybe find a well-paying job within corporate America.

The very idea of success is so deeply personal, and so varied, that it's difficult to make any generalized observations. Nevertheless, I will make a few. The first is that the biggest barrier to success is the fear of failure. This fear may prevent us from even *trying* to succeed because we dwell on the consequences of failure. This is innate in human nature (see discussion of Prospect theory in the Making Decisions essay). Humans anticipate feeling badly due to failure, so are unwilling to take risks. As the saying goes, "you miss 100% of the shots you never take." I wish I could offer a magical solution to this issue, but I have none. I can suggest that failure is usually not as dire as we imagine. We will not be judged as harshly as we imagine, and the consequences of failure are often far less than we fear. In fact, it is a cliche that we learn more from our failures than our successes, so trying and failing is a necessary part of growth. In fact, the people I tend to avoid in my own life are those who have had an unbroken string of successes. In my experience, they lack empathy for others and tend to believe that anyone can succeed as they have, if they only try. Often, they have been lucky and fail to acknowledge the role luck plays in all our lives.

There is another, more subtle, aspect of the fear of failure. We sometimes feel the need to stay on a path even when success is unlikely (or even when we realize we no longer wish to achieve the goal). Mt Everest has claimed over 330 lives since people began climbing it a hundred years ago. Either because they were so driven to succeed (or so afraid to fail), these climbers pressed on even when it should have been clear that their ascent was unlikely to succeed. In less dramatic examples, people sometimes stay in

11

careers they don't enjoy because they imagine outside pressure to prove they can succeed at it, even when they realize that they themselves no longer desire success in that field. There are many famous, successful people who gained their greatest success in their second (or third) career: Julia Child (from government spy agency to advertising to French chef), Ray Kroc (milkshake machine salesman to fast food franchiser) and Vera Wang (figure skater to journalist to fashion designer) are just a few examples. If these people had all stuck to their original careers for fear of striding into completely new pursuits, they likely never would have become famous.

Speaking of fame, I personally have never understood the desire to be famous. While there are some benefits of fame, no doubt, fame also brings a loss of anonymity, which many famous people say is a very high price to pay. Fans have a sense of ownership of celebrities and are quick to disapprove when celebrities behave in ways they disapprove of. Many celebrities have had their career derailed by a bad exchange with a service provider or a bad date or a thoughtless post to social media. As for posthumous fame, I think I can prove that it is worthless. Either there is no life after death, in which case one would never know they are famous amongst the living, or there is. If there is some sort of heaven, I would imagine the heavenly multitudes would be too busy singing God's praises (or whatever they will be doing) than to worry about how they are being discussed down on Earth.

The desire for riches is a bit more understandable. At least, one should strive to avoid poverty, which does tend to correlate with unhappiness. People do seem to be happier as wealth increases. Life expectancy also increases with wealth. But both trends flatten and have ceilings at about the top 5% of incomes. So, striving to be the richest person on the planet does not seem to be a worthwhile endeavor.

In many studies of happiness, the things that do seem to correlate with happiness are the depth of our personal relationships and our sense of purpose. Having close social connections with friends and family; people who know you well and respect and admire you, brings a sense of self-worth that far exceeds the admiration of strangers. I have often thought how empty it must feel for some famous people to have crowds adoring them; people who are really strangers, but then to have lives that are isolated and lonely. There are many stories of the rich and famous dying alone in their mansions or hotel suites, Elvis being just one infamous example.

So, success can mean different things to different people, but it pays to ensure the type of success you are pursuing is what will truly make you happy. And, in pursuing that success, we must be prepared to fail at times and overcome our natural fears that would otherwise lead to a sense of regret at missed opportunities.

Making Decisions

"There are three kinds of lies: lies, damned lies, and statistics" - Mark Twain

Human beings make approximately 20,000 decisions every day, most as a matter of routine. However, occasionally we are confronted with major decisions that could impact the course of our lives. Such decisions, once made, often cannot be undone. As a result, humans tend to spend a lot of time (likely too much time) going over past decisions. This is because life can be like moving up a tree. We begin at the base of the tree, with the option to progress up the tree in almost any direction. But, as we choose path after path, we find ourselves with ever fewer options as to where we will end up. That is because each choice necessarily rejects alternate routes, leaving us at one corner of the tree in its outermost branches. I believe this is what Robert Frost was referring to in his magnificent poem, "The Road Not Taken": "Two roads diverged in a wood, and I - I took the one less traveled by, And that has made all the difference."

So, given the importance of certain decisions, how can we optimize our decision making? Before I delve into techniques for making better decisions, let me first note that people can sometimes put too much emphasis on their choices. Usually, the successful execution of a decision can be more important than the choice itself. Think of choosing a career. Likely, there is more than one career that can be a good match for a person's interests and skills. If they approach their career with determination, hard work and a bit of luck, then there are likely several careers which a person might find rewarding. Other choices are similar. So, one trick to making decisions, as opposed to getting mired in indecision, is to realize that we are often choosing between equally workable alternatives. That is why I have always wished I could go back in time and make other choices. Not because I am dissatisfied with any choices I've made, but curious about where alternatives would have led.

Daniel Kahneman in his book, Thinking Fast and Slow, identified two types of decision making, which he calls System 1 and System 2. System 1 represents thinking fast. It is our intuitive decision-making process designed to make quick, usually routine decisions (e.g., whether to stop at a red light). System 2 represents thinking slow. It's used when we want to carefully consider an important or unusual decision. However, our senses can absorb 11 million bits of information every second, but our brain can only process

16 bits a second. Not 16 million bits or 16 thousand bits, but 16. As a result, most of our decisions are made reflexively, without conscious thought. Often, even when we think we've decided consciously, all we've really done is use our conscious brain to rationalize a decision we made reflexively. That is what the quotation at the start of this essay is partially commenting on: that we use statistics to obscure the truth rather than illuminate it.

Most of the time, this split decision-making process works adequately. It works especially well when we confront the sorts of decisions we evolved to confront (e.g., flee or fight a predator). However, because we live in a very different world than we evolved to live in, our decision-making heuristics can exhibit characteristics that are unhelpful in achieving our goals. Kahneman and his research partner, Amos Tversky, conducted controlled studies to identify these heuristics. They include 1) finding patterns when there are none; 2) utilizing irrelevant information when making decisions; 3) over-relying on previous mental models (bias); 4) over-generalizing from very small samples; 5) taking on excess risk to avoid a negative outcome; and 6) overestimating the chances of a positive outcome. These last two heuristics are part of Prospect Theory, for which Kahneman received the Nobel Prize in Economics in 2002.

Simply put, Prospect Theory states that people feel losses more acutely than an equivalent gain which drives behavior that is sometimes irrational.

One last point on the gap between how we evolved and how we live today: our moral compass can also be compromised. People usually have a strong (and correct) reaction to things like physical violence. This innate sense of aversion to the strong attacking the weak, especially children, makes sense both in the wilds in which humans evolved and, in our society, today. However, people often have a less instinctive aversion to cyber theft, which can be just as damaging to its victims. That is because there is no primitive equivalent to financial crimes against strangers. This "modern" morality must be learned just as treating people fairly, even when they look quite different from us, must be learned. An evolved morality will be somewhat contrary to the instinctive reactions inherited from our distant ancestors, so simply relying on our first impulses may not yield the correct responses.

Given the pitfalls of System 1 decision making, how can we make better decisions? The first challenge is to recognize when we have an important decision to make and engage System 2. This is more difficult than it may first seem. We make so many decisions during the day, and System 1 is so very much the default decision-making habit, that we can sometimes miss the importance of decisions we are making as we make them. As an example, think about people who decide to stay in their home when they have been warned to evacuate because of an impending major storm. People tend to instinctively feel comfortable in their home. Using System 1, they may fall prey to believing because their home has not been flooded in the past, it won't be flooded now (over-generalizing from small samples, overestimating the chances of a positive outcome). So, they decide to stay, despite government warnings, and end up nearly drowning. This was an important decision that they should have considered more methodically instead of relying on their gut instinct.

In my career I was often amazed by how otherwise intelligent professionals would quickly react to critical decisions and take the path that seemed most hopeful (or least onerous). Certainly, some famous white-collar crimes started by seemingly mundane choices. For example, Bernie Madoff made a fateful decision to borrow some client funds to provide above market returns to another client as a "temporary" solution, and ultimately ended up overseeing the largest Ponzi scheme in history.

Assuming the challenge of recognizing an important decision has been overcome, how to engage in a useful decision-making process? There are several inherent problems with complex decisions: 1) the variables and parameters are often unknown; 2) the decision may require many inputs from multiple stakeholders, perspectives and disciplines; 2) the decision may require long-term predictions of the future; 4) there may be varied levels of uncertainty, including aspects that we have not identified; 5) there may be conflicting objectives (e.g., professional vs. personal); 6) we need to identify options as of yet undiscovered; 7) we may still be prone to System 1 heuristics without realizing it (e.g., loss aversion); and 8) if deciding with others, we may fall victim to "group think." It is beyond the scope of this essay to address all these issues in detail. I would recommend Steven Johnson's book, Farsighted, for a more detailed discussion of these challenges in making complex decisions as well as a process for making complex decisions that addresses these challenges.

I would like to address the one aspect I have found to be most common: falling into the trap of binary decision making. Far too often I have found people limit themselves to the options put in front of them. For example, sign the apartment lease or look for another place to live; or accept the job offer or move on. These two options are seldom all that are available. The trick is to 1) determine what other options there are and 2) have the courage to put these better options forward in a negotiation. A common example would be an apartment lease. Often people assume that any contract put in front of them cannot be negotiated, so their reaction is to not to even bother to read it before they sign. They underestimate the landlord's desire to get a tenant, and their potential willingness to accommodate reasonable requests. An example might be providing more notice before entering the apartment. Having the creativity to consider alternatives and the courage to put these forward can open up a whole new set of options: the "win-win" scenarios vs. the usual "win-lose" outcomes.

The trick is how to identify these alternative options. Techniques include such things as considering that the preferred path is unavailable and forcing yourself to come up with alternatives. Another option is to "throw out" the first several ideas to force the group to dig deeper to mine more original approaches. A third option is to consider extreme options that at first seemed impractical and think harder at how they might be made to work. The extra work may well be worth it. Studies have shown that new options improve satisfaction with outcomes by over 50%. Developing a habit of considering options "outside the box" can improve not only your own outcomes, but the satisfaction of the others impacted by your choices.

Money

"Wealth consists not in having great possessions, but in having few wants" – Epictetus

"I love money. I love everything about it. I bought some pretty good stuff. Got me a $300 pair of socks. Got a fur sink. An electric dog polisher. A gasoline powered turtleneck sweater. And, of course, I bought some dumb stuff, too." - Steve Martin

When I was living in Japan at the age of 27, I was asked to be the treasurer of Tokyo Union Church, which was a large ecumenical church in Tokyo that catered to the international and Japanese Christian community in the fashionable neighborhood of Omotesando, Tokyo. When I objected that I wasn't qualified because I was too young and had never been a church treasurer, the elder for finance stated that I was qualified because I did not have "magical thinking" about money.

I have often thought about this conversation since, because I think he was right. I find that many people think about money emotionally rather than mathematically.

Myths about money abound from money comes to the pious to money is a tool of the Devil. Money can be a source of prestige, or power, or status, or happiness. Many people think that more money will solve their problems and that certain institutions, like the government, their employer, or their church, can draw on infinite amounts of money at will. People who have money don't deserve it, and people who deserve money can't get it (sometimes these last two are true).

The main point is that money is just a tool, like a nail, or any tool. If you don't have it when you need it, then you will feel its absence. But having more nails than you need doesn't really do much good. You could go around putting extra nails everywhere, but it won't improve your life.

I once read a study of lottery winners. They are amongst the most unhappy people. Before their winnings, they had a stable life with friends and family (and challenges). After they won, they found that the people they knew all felt that they should receive a constant stream of gifts, so their relationships broke down. However, they did not really have the life experiences of typically wealthy people, so they had difficulty making friends within their new class. The usual result was divorce, loneliness and ultimate bankruptcy. The happiest lottery winners are those that somehow can return to their old lives.

Of course, one's perspective about money depends a great deal on whether you are able to meet your basic needs, and I am certainly not suggesting that we don't need money. We need enough money to be able to be free from the stress of losing our home or having enough to eat. It cannot be ignored that wealth distribution in the US is systematically and dramatically unequal. Many people, through no fault of their own, will struggle to make enough money to meet their necessities for their entire lives. A 2023 survey by SecureSave found that 63% of employed Americans could not afford a $500 emergency expense. There are things that should be changed in the American economy to ensure that all workers are paid a living wage.

However, I am suggesting that income alone is not the solution to all personal financial issues. Over one third of Americans making $100,000 or more a year were found to be living paycheck-to-paycheck. Part of the solution, for those people that can manage enough income for necessities, may be balancing their wants with their resources and it is usually as easy to reduce the one as increase the other.

I was raised in a solid middle-class household. My parents, each of whom were the first in their families to attend college, believed in living below their means. This allowed them to save for emergencies and, in the case of my father, retire early. From my own privileged position as someone who has been able to make a good income through my working life, I have found that if you can manage to spend less than you make, investing your money over time can become both a source of future security and future income. Many people underestimate the long-term costs of debt and the long-term benefits of investing. The truly wealthy earn more from their money than from their labor.

The goal for money in your life is that you do not want it to secure too large a place in your thoughts. Hopefully, you can practice enough frugality in your life that you are satisfied with what you are able to achieve financially. If you focus on money as a tool that requires planning and math, not a magical salvation, you will be able to think about money less and focus on the things that really can make you happy.

Work Life

"Unfortunately, the sort of individual who is programmed to keep pushing for the top is frequently programmed to disregard signs of grave and imminent danger as well." - John Krakauer, <u>Into Thin Air</u>

For many people, their work becomes the vehicle for their ambitions. Not all people. Some people are driven by a desire to help humanity or create art or other ambitions. But for many, work offers easily measured milestones of ambition: salary, titles and other perks. Humans are very status conscious - it's in our DNA. If you look at troops of monkeys or apes, they spend their lives primarily in the pursuit (or maintenance) of status. Therefore, it's very easy for people to become focused on rising in their level at work; it's a default. However, one often finds that people at the very top of their fields, whether that be corporations, politics or even art forms, have often sacrificed their relationships along the way. For example, studies have shown that CEOs have greater levels of social isolation and higher levels of divorce than ordinary people (they also have much higher rates of psychopathy, but that would be a different essay). This gets back to the idea that our natural behaviors and desires are not necessarily aligned with our happiness.

I think one of the great challenges of human life is recognizing those desires which are really vestiges of our more primitive selves and making a conscious choice to regulate those desires to achieve a higher level of happiness and purpose.

None of the above is intended to disparage ambition absolutely, however. A complete lack of ambition is also detrimental and can lead to a life without a feeling of purpose. And a sense of purpose is necessary for happiness. Plus, achievement can be very rewarding. The challenge, as in much of life, is to find balance. And, while studies have shown that ever greater levels of financial resources do not lead to higher rates of happiness, a lack of adequate resources can lead to unhappiness. Again, we should be aiming for something in between an unambitious, unsuccessful lay about relying on charity and becoming the most famous or wealthy person in the world. The question is not "How far can I go in my career?", but rather "How far do I want to go in my career in order to still have balance?" The answer to this question will evolve over time and change with our changing lives and priorities. The most important thing is to consciously consider the question vs. simply falling into a pattern of striving for ever more success.

This leads to another question: "How much do we sacrifice for our work? "Again, we should strive for balance. And again, regularly asking ourselves this question is more important than any given answer. Simple awareness of the need for balance will help shape our actions. There is a natural tension between the demands of success (e.g., intense focus and long hours) and the demands of a balanced life (e.g., nurturing our important relationships and maintaining our physical and mental health). For me, the demands of my family offered a natural counter-tension to the demands of my work. My company would have me working 16 hours a day, while my wife wanted me home to help raise our children. Trying to disappoint neither party offered me the tension that was critical in achieving some sort of balance. So, relationships may be critical in achieving work-life balance. Without them, there may be no counterweight to the demands of ambition, which will only lead to further isolation and ultimate unhappiness.

Navigating Relationships

So, Scorpion jumped onto Frog's back and Frog began to swim across the river. But halfway across, Scorpion took his deadly sting and stuck it into Frog's back. And as the poison filled Frog's body his arms began to stiffen and they both began to sink. "Why?" gasped Frog in despair.

"Sorry Frog," said Scorpion. "It's my nature."

"The Scorpion and the Frog" - Russian fable

In my youth, I believed in the essential goodness of all people. I believed that even people who behaved badly would happily renounce their evil deeds if a person could simply make them aware of how their actions negatively impacted others. I thought that all my relationships would ultimately succeed, if only I invested sufficient energy into them.

Most readers already have concluded that my youthful perspective was hopelessly naive. Yet, I held onto this view until my senior year in college. As a leader of a student organization, I encountered some fellow students who quite clearly sought to take advantage of the organization and their fellow students to get something for nothing. They bounced checks, shirked responsibilities, went with us to out-of-town trips (but did not participate in the scheduled events) and just generally behaved in extremely selfish ways. When confronted, they had no interest or concern about the impact they had on other students or the organization. Their complete lack of concern shocked me into re-evaluating my naive outlook.

Over the course of my career, I came to specialize in dealing with situations resulting from selfish, unethical and sometimes illegal behavior. I also suffered frustration in some of my personal relationships from betrayals, indifference and falseness. While I had long ago abandoned my naive belief in the goodness of all mankind, I now began to ask myself a different question. What portion of people behave badly and why?

Now, I should caveat the following observations with the fact that I have no data to support any of what follows. My observations are purely anecdotal. However, I would offer that I have dealt extensively with all nature of human weaknesses, at least those possible to encounter in the context of business. My role as a risk officer for my firm meant I often had to be involved with various bad actors, both within the firm and at clients. I have encountered most crimes on the books, not just financial crimes, but outright thefts and even sexual assault. I have extensively researched the details of many frauds and been intimately involved in the resolution of several very high-profile corporate frauds. I have also lectured on the topic of why certain people perpetuate frauds.

My belief is that, with respect to integrity, people fall onto a bell curve. This is hardly revolutionary thinking in that people fall on a bell curve distribution for most things one can measure. What this means in practical terms is that a small percentage of people will always attempt to do what they believe to be right, regardless of who is or is not watching and regardless of the consequences. Conversely, there is a small percentage of people that one might label as "evil" who will consistently lie, cheat and steal regardless of whether they are likely to face consequences (perhaps they act without considering consequences). I would estimate each of these groups to consist of between 5-10% of people, hoping that the "good" group is on the high end and the "evil" group is on the lower end, but I am not as certain as I am hopeful. Most people, however, will consider the possible consequences, and some will be tempted to do the wrong thing if they are certain there are no consequences, while others will be more risk tolerant and will do the wrong thing if they think there is a chance the reward will outweigh the cost. These folks will also fall along a bell-curve spectrum. So, at one end, the wrong actions people are willing to undertake may be very minor (e.g., speeding), or they will only be tempted to do wrong if the reward is great. Others might be tempted to do great wrong for relatively minor rewards. I have also observed that when the consequences are sufficiently severe, many people will turn on even close friends to save themselves. The phenomenon of a drowning man drowning his would-be rescuer applies to white collar criminals as well.

As an aside, I have a couple of observations from the above related to the workplace: 1) People often overestimate the support they will have from their "friends" within their employer's organization in investigations. Most people, when given a choice of preserving their own job or assisting their friend against their mutual employer's interests, will choose to preserve their position with their employer. Many people have been shocked by how easily their work friends will abandon them when such choices are presented. Therefore, one should always be cautious about what they reveal to coworker friends, especially their own misconduct or severe criticisms of management. 2) I have sometimes been in positions where I was responsible for over 100 employees. I had an expression "a little fear is a good thing."

My meaning is that a manager wants to create an environment where people feel comfortable, but not complacent. A sense of accountability is important for any team to function at a high level. A good manager does not play favorites based upon personal relationships, only performance. When I have become friends with subordinates, it was only after I was highly confident that they were strong performers and that any friendships would not negatively impact that.

People are also more likely to follow laws and rules that they find reasonable/understand vs. laws or rules they disagree with or don't understand the purpose. It is important that society and organizations establish controls to make people feel that there will be consequences because studies have shown that this impacts people's decisions. I believe that the percentage of people who may steal a large sum if they think they can get away with it is not small, maybe 30%-50% or more, so the existence of these controls is important, not only for the organization, but to help people resist temptation, possibly damaging their own lives irreparably.

In contrast to my youthful faith, I believe most adults' moral compasses are relatively fixed. So, if a person habitually lies, cheats or steals, one should expect them to continue to lie, cheat or steal. The only thing that changes is their assessment of the consequences. This is relevant in evaluating whether to continue in relationships, as a partner who has lied to you, cheated on you, or otherwise treated you poorly should be expected to continue to do so. As per the fable, it is their nature, and they likely cannot help themselves. I am not saying people are irredeemable, nor that people don't sometimes make mistakes that they regret. But, if you have a relationship with someone that makes a habit of disrespecting or disappointing you, you are better off cutting bait than persisting in hoping they will change. In my experience, they likely won't. I have dealt with people who have put their livelihoods at risk over and over, even when they knew that another transgression would result in their dismissal. Like the scorpion in the story, they cannot help themselves, even when their actions are not in their own interests. If they someday find a path to reforming themselves, good for them, but you are better off keeping your eyes wide open for your own protection than giving a person of bad faith another opportunity to harm you.

God and Religion

"If God did not exist, it would be necessary to invent him"
- Voltaire

I think we often ask the wrong question relating to God and religion. Rather than, "does God exist?" we should be asking "does God and religion play a useful role in human society?". Or, perhaps, "does religion have anything to offer me in my own life?"

Firstly, I think it's impossible to prove that God does not exist. Although there are atheists who are convinced there is no God, they must exercise nearly as much faith as those who unquestionably believe in God. It is impossible for us mere mortals to completely understand the entirety of the universe. Although we have certainly made giant strides in the past few centuries in terms of our understanding of the natural laws of the universe, as our knowledge increases, we often realize that previous scientific facts are disproven or found incomplete. Just one example would be the progression from Newtonian physics to Quantum mechanics and other systems which followed that. Each version was correct in that it could explain many

natural phenomena, but we later learned that these explanations were incomplete. So, while I think it highly unlikely
that God as represented in the major religions is accurate,
the possibility that there are god-like forces in the universe
beyond our understanding remains.

Another point to consider when it comes to the existence of anything "supernatural" is that we need to re-
member that our senses are very limited. Our senses
evolved to help us survive the ancient plains of Africa. Any
trait that did not contribute to that survival was not likely to
be selected. This means that there are many sounds we cannot hear, much of the light spectrum we cannot see, mag-
netic fields we cannot perceive, etc. Therefore, our percep-
tion of the world is dramatically limited. So, anything we
cannot readily perceive might have been labeled as "supernatural" by our ancestors. And while their explanations
might be flawed, that does not negate the existence of real-
ities we simply cannot perceive with our limited senses.
That does not of course mean that there is a traditional, Bib-
lical God in the heavens, but that could mean that there are
forces at work in the universe that we do not fully understand. An analogy is how we understand an electronic de-
vice like a computer or smartphone. We think we under-

stand it because we interact with it successfully, but that interface has been built for our convenience. Our ability to use it says nothing for our understanding of it, because below the interface we think we understand, is a series of binary computations performed on microchips of which most people know virtually nothing. Similarly, because we interact with the physical world daily, in no way implies we understand how it actually works.

Another objection to the existence of God is the various religions and their disagreements as to the "one true God". How can there be a "true" God if every religion disagrees about the details? I once heard a sermon by the then dean of Grace Cathedral in San Francisco, Alan Jones. He introduced me to the idea of religious pluralism by providing what has now become a common illustration of the validity of different religions. If one provides directions to climb a mountain, the directions will differ depending on the starting point. If the west side of the mountain was a forest, and the south side a desert and the north side a tundra, and so on, then the climbing directions would have to differ for each group depending on their departure point. In the same way, each religion provides a path to God, but given the cultural, historical and geographical differences between peoples, there cannot be but one path. Therefore, the differences in religions does not invalidate the existence of God (or of each other), these differences merely reflect the differences between pilgrims (and so we should stop fighting about who is right).

So, how to respond to religion as an agnostic, then? To that I would say that it doesn't really matter whether the God of the Hebrew/Christian Bible exists or not. As the Voltaire quote above implies, there are many societal benefits to the existence of God, one of which is the idea of a transcendent morality, and ultimate accountability. But I believe there is also benefit for the individual. Firstly, a book like the Bible (or the Koran or other ancient religious texts) does not survive for thousands of years without having something to say about the human condition. Personally, I have always been partial to the book of Ecclesiastes: "I returned, and saw under the sun, that the race is not to the swift, nor the battle to the strong, neither yet bread to the wise, nor yet riches to men of understanding, nor yet favor to men of skill; but time and chance happen to them all." 9:11. I have yet to find a single sentence that summarizes the human condition better than that. Secondly, if we look to the New Testament as a book of philosophy rather than the Word of God, there is still much to admire. We can even admire it as a beautiful work of literature. How many weddings recite the First Corinthians definition of love? "Love is patient, love is kind. It does not envy, it does not boast, it is not proud. It does not dishonor others, it is not self-seeking, it is not easily angered, it keeps no record of wrongs. Love does not delight in evil but rejoices with the truth. It always protects, always trusts, always hopes, always perseveres." 13:4-8. I am sure many of the newlyweds may not be true believers, but how better can we define the kind of love we all wish for at the start of a lifetime partnership?

I would argue that, even beyond these reasons, gathering in a community of people of faith and good will is good for one's spiritual development and mental health. Sharing with people who recognize that they fall short of an ideal for human interaction, but are committed to moving closer to realizing the teachings of Jesus; teachings that focus on love and forgiveness, how can that not be a good thing? I am certainly not arguing that religion is not often misused. It's undeniable. However, I would submit that the failings we associate with religion are almost always the failings of the institutions, leaders and congregants of the religion, not the philosophy of the religion. We find such failings in all human institutions, be they political, economic or charitable. So, a religious organization is certainly no guarantee against self-service or hypocrisy. If one were to reject all human activity because all are subject to corruption and hijacking by grifters, then one would have to live a life of isolation, with negative impacts on both the individual and the society.

I speak primarily of Christianity, because I am most familiar with that. However, what I do know of Judaism, Islam and Buddhism would also support the idea that what these religions prescribe for interactions between people and the universe are often very noble reactions to an imperfect world. If all the adherents were truly able to follow the teachings of their prophets, the stain on religion that so many people see today would likely not be there.

My own experience, which involved moving to new cities every 3-5 years, indicates that joining a church has been a very effective strategy to quickly integrate into a new community. Church congregations, though many are in decline, are quick to welcome new members. Churches can also afford one the opportunity to become involved in charitable endeavors, many of which are secular in nature.

In his essay, "Bowling Alone: America's Declining Social Capital", Robert Putnam discusses the nature and consequences of declining community involvement by Americans. Churches and religion have been a place in America where people got together and formed relationships, often across political, class and (sometimes) racial lines ("bridging social capital" in the language of Putnam). Churches have also acted as meeting places for important civic and personal events (e.g., weddings and funerals). In this way, in its ideal form, religion has been one of the anchors to community involvement (although admittedly religion has also been a source of community division at times). So, not just the philosophy of religions, but the physical infrastructure, can act as a source of building the social capital America so desperately needs.

I believe that, once we free ourselves of the need to prove or disprove the existence of God, we can evaluate a religion based on its contributions to society and to us as an individual. One definition of "sacred" is "worthy of awe and respect." Certainly, a philosophy and organization built around the idea of loving thy neighbor fulfills that definition.

Desire

"...it is easier to suppress the first desire than to satisfy all that follow it" -Ben Franklin

In A Picture of Dorian Gray, one of the main characters gives the following advice: "The only way to get rid of a temptation is to yield to it. Resist it, and your soul grows sick with longing for the things it has forbidden to itself..." One might argue that Oscar Wilde followed this advice, to his detriment. However, I have come to believe that human appetites (as opposed to needs) can be ignored without great consequence. True needs (e.g., breathing, hydration) cannot be ignored. Denying these creates ever greater dissonance until we either satisfy them, fall unconscious, or die. Appetites can seem compelling when they first arise. However, they will ultimately lessen, whether we satisfy them or not.

For several years I fasted two days a week, taking in less than 500 calories each fasting day. Of course, I became hungry. I had been raised to eat whenever I was hungry, such that I thought it a requirement. However, through fasting I came to realize that eventually the hunger subsided whether or not I ate. Of course, one must eat eventually, but a human can go several days without eating, if necessary.

In fact, there are some studies to show it may be healthier to fast than to eat whenever hungry (which can lead to obesity). One can easily imagine that our prehistoric ancestors often had to go days without much to eat, yet they survived. While the body and mind want to eat, we evolved in an environment where it might not be possible to eat a large meal every few hours. It would be too distracting to our survival if hunger simply escalated ad infinitum until it consumed our every waking thought.

In considering this experience, I came to realize that most all desires behave in the same manner. You may desire luxury, you may desire possessions, you may desire a romance with an infatuation, you may desire status, you may desire various vices like drugs or alcohol. However, as Ben Franklin suggests, attempting to satisfy these desires may actually *increase* the desire rather than sate it. The more rich desserts we eat, the more cigarettes we smoke, the more wealth we obtain; they all simply set up the next desire for more of the same. Alternatively, if we resist these initial desires, quite unlike Oscar Wilde's advice, the perceived need for these things decreases. Not right away of course. It might take days or even weeks, but eventually an unfulfilled desire will eventually fade. Counterintuitively, our attempts to satisfy our desires will offer temporary, but only temporary relief from them.

Psalm 23 begins with its familiar "the Lord is my shepherd; I shall not want." It is clear as one reads the full psalm that the Lord is not showering the author with riches ("Yea, though I walk through the valley of the shadow of death, I will fear no evil"). Rather, the author's faith in God has made him immune to the petty desires of each day. It is this spiritual contentment, rather than an endless pursuit after every desire, that leads ultimately to happiness. We must cultivate "a satisfied mind" as the Joe Hayes song suggests. Then we will be truly rich.

Leadership

Jesus called them together and said, "You know that the rulers of the Gentiles lord it over them, and their high officials exercise authority over them. Not so with you. Instead, whoever wants to become great among you must be your servant, and whoever wants to be first must be your slave—just as the Son of Man did not come to be served, but to serve, and to give his life as a ransom for many." - Matthew 20:25-28

As I note elsewhere in these pages, one does not have to believe in the divinity of Jesus nor the divine nature of the Bible to recognize that it has endured for over 2,000 years. There is also evidence of the existence of a historical Jesus. So, at a minimum, the Bible speaks to the constancy of the human condition. I would also argue that the two types of leadership Jesus identifies in this passage are essentially the same two types of leadership that exist today.

Leadership stems from some sort of power: wealth, status, ideas, charisma, etc. This power is used by the leader either for his or her own aggrandizement or on behalf of those led. The latter is referred to in modern business as "servant leadership." The first style of leadership, or traditional leadership, I define as "lazy leadership." It is lazy because it comes naturally to humans. For some people, their entire lives are a quest for status. This is embedded in our DNA; monkeys and other apes spend their whole lives trying to move up the social pecking order. So, seeking to self-aggrandize is basically autopilot for human behavior and Jesus describes this as the behavior of the Gentiles (a bit unfairly perhaps) in wanting to "lord it over" their followers. I should note here that I am not intending this essay to be a religious essay, but Jesus actually represents the earliest appearance of a servant leader in human literature, so I am going to continue to draw examples from these writings about his life and philosophy. The term "servant leader" was first used in 1970 in an essay by Robert Greenleaf, but there are other historical examples of leaders who defined their rule in terms of service (e.g., Frederick II of Prussia).

But if lazy leadership is easy and apparently rewarding for the leader, why consider servant leadership? Servant leadership is much more work. It involves sharing power and credit. It requires putting the needs of followers before the needs of the leader. It involves a focus on the development of the followers. This sounds like a lot of work and sacrifice!

Lazy leadership always uses, to some degree, fear as its primary motivator. This can be as extreme as fear of punishment or as subtle as fear of being excluded from the inner circle and the resulting loss of status. But such a leadership style inevitably involves the followers' direct relationship with their leader. They either seek to have the favor of the leader (e.g., a royal court), or to escape the notice of the leader (e.g., a slave whose only interaction with their master usually involves punishment). This means that the goals of the leader and the goals of the lead are not in alignment. Whatever the leader's goals; the followers' goals are only to be *perceived* as advancing the leader's goals. This usually results in followers trying to shape the perceptions of the leader inaccurately, to be perceived as contributing more than they actually do to the leader's objectives. The follower's status, which is their primary focus, depends only upon the leader's perceptions, not the reality. This can result in the leader having a wholly inaccurate picture of the conditions of their organization (or country or whatever). There are countless examples of leaders making terrible decisions because of this gap in their knowledge between the actual and perceived conditions. Think of a king whose people revolt. These revolts are usually due to the king's massive misperception of the mood of his people.

Another disadvantage of the lazy style of leadership is that the goals of the leader usually do not last beyond the leader's time in power. Because the followers merely want to be perceived as aligned with the leader, they may not have internalized the leader's goals. They will agree with the leader's objectives only as long as he or she is in place to monitor their reactions. Even if they do agree with the leader's objectives, because lazy leadership does not emphasize developing the follower's skills (in fact, this may be contrary to the leader's interests as these followers could potentially replace the leader), the followers may not have the ability to further the leader's goals without the leader's guidance.

Finally, because in a lazy leadership structure, every party is motivated by their own selfish interests, there is an incentive for the followers to replace the leader. Since the lazy leader has the highest status, and status is the goal of the members of the group, it is natural for the followers to covet the leader's status. Also, because fear is at the core of the motivation of this leadership style, the only way for a follower to eliminate their fear is to replace the leader (although they usually find that the fear of punishment is now replaced by the fear of replacement). In a kingdom, these actions can be extreme (e.g., death as a punishment for treason or beheading of a king replaced in palace coup), these fundamental concepts exist even in modern corporations (e.g., workers who are demoted or fired as punishment and leaders who are secretly undermined by their employees).

The life of Jesus provides an excellent example of the benefits of the servant leadership style. First and foremost, the motivation for his followers was not fear, but love ("A new command I give you: Love one another. As I have loved you, so you must love one another." John 13:34). Now a boss may not "love" all their employees (or they her), but terms like "respect" "admire" or "mentor" are often appropriate in these servant-leader relationships. There are several significant advantages in these relationships over the lazy style of leadership. First, because the followers often admire, or at least respect, their leader, it is likely that they will feel more ownership towards the leader's objectives. This would imply they will work towards those objectives, even when "not being watched." Secondly, the leader is much more likely to have accurate information than in the case of the more traditional leader. This is because people in the organization will know that even "bad news" will likely be greeted with collaborative problem solving vs. punishment, which means that problems can be safely brought forward. And, of course, a leadership style characterized by mutual respect, even love, hardly encourages the kind of zero-sum competition within the group that more traditional leadership styles foster. This lack of competition with the leader and within the team is the origin of the cliche that states: "A players hire A players, but B players hire C players."

Most importantly, because the leader is focused on developing the others in the organization, it is more likely that the work will be carried forward in the leader's absence, both because the followers share the leader's goals and because they have been provided the skills necessary to move the work forward on their own. We see this constantly in the examples between Jesus and his followers. Jesus is often referred to as rabbi (teacher) by his Disciples and there are many examples of Jesus instructing the Disciples in various matters throughout the New Testament. Indeed, the New Testament documents the work of many of the Disciples after Jesus' death, and the ultimate result is that Christianity becomes arguably the most successful religion in the world's history. So, judging purely by the results, Jesus' leadership style was incredibly effective.

Power

"Nothing discloses real character like the use of power. It is easy for the weak to be gentle. Most people can bear adversity. But if you wish to know what a man really is, give him power. This is the supreme test." - Robert Ingersoll writing about Abraham Lincoln

Virtually all people want power. This usually begins as a desire for a child to have power over themselves, because their parents control a great deal of what happens in a child's life. As a child reaches adolescence, they push against parental control in a very natural desire to have the power to make their own choices. However, because humans are essentially hierarchical in their social structures, this desire for power over oneself often morphs into a desire for power over others. More power equates to more social status because, of course, those over whom you have power will often seek to ingratiate themselves with you to protect themselves.

There are two basic types of power: hard power and soft power. Hard power tends towards the coercive (e.g., do what I wish or suffer punishment). Soft power is about influence. Perhaps a person is attractive (this could be physical but can also be intangibles, like their social status, ideas, values, or lifestyle). People wish to be associated with the holder of soft power to enjoy the same admiration as the wielder of such power. A person wielding soft power uses their ability to shape perceptions and create favorable impressions to gain their objectives. A key difference is that soft power can be either active or passive, while hard power is almost always active. In other words, a wielder of hard power needs to actively exert that power (or at least threaten to), while an owner of soft power often influences those whom they are not attempting to influence (they may not even know those subject to their power). An example might be a role model, where others try to emulate her example, even though she may not have this as an objective. Indeed, a famous role model likely influences people they have never met.

Often people who have newly come into power tend to default to using hard power, as its relationship between the use of power and desired outcomes is direct and easily understood. However, hard power often tends to diminish the more it is used. It often engenders active resistance, because people do not wish to be further forced into actions they did not choose. Another way it diminishes is that the actual exercise of hard power is often less effective than either side expected. An example is a punishment that, once meted out, is not as difficult to withstand as either side feared beforehand. Intentionally or not, the object of the hard power exercise calls the powerful person's bluff, so to speak, and finds that they are indeed capable of withstanding the consequences.

Soft power, by contrast, does not typically create resistance, and therefore does not diminish when exercised (as discussed above, its exercise may be passive). In fact, soft power can increase with use. Think of the role model whose followers grow as they also benefit from the association. Another example would be a cultural artist whose influence expands as more people come to appreciate him. Therefore, soft power can be much more impactful than hard power over time. The negative aspect may be that it's harder to control the timing and impact of soft power.

As per the quote about Lincoln at the top of this essay, while people desire power, careful exercise can be a challenge for people. As with many temptations, power tempts people to use it selfishly, for their own benefit. This likely will cause resentment by others and can ultimately result in the loss of all power (or in the case of despots, even their lives). Selfish use of power is often hard power, which tends to diminish with use. Using soft power for the greater good will often increase one's influence, even beyond a lifetime. Think of Martin Luther King's ideas that still reverberate through the culture many years after his passing. In that way, a person's active use of hard power can be counterproductive over the long term while the positive use of soft power can result in an increase of influence over the long term.

A tangential observation regarding people who achieve power is that authoritative figures will usually be granted an undue amount of deference (at least for a while). Stanley Milgram's famous experiments of the early 1960s showed that subjects were willing to take actions they believed could kill other volunteers based simply upon instructions from a researcher in a lab coat they had just met. I believe this stems from an assumption that people with power deserve it somehow, either by being smarter, wiser, more noble or otherwise superior to average people. I have had the opportunity to work with many powerful people: CEOs of large corporations, for example. I have found that, while they are not stupid, they are not necessarily superior in their motivations from ordinary people. They are as likely to act for their own selfish interests as anyone, maybe more than most. Because even those people that go into roles with the best of intentions tend to be corrupted by power over time. As Aung San Suu Kyi famously observed "It is not power that corrupts but fear. Fear of losing power corrupts those who wield it." Many people come to identify so strongly with their position of authority, that they will do almost anything to preserve it. The common element for most people who obtain power is not their higher moral values, but their shared desire to wield power.

As an interesting aside, the dynamics observed in human behavior relative to power are not different from human organizations' desire for power. Nation states, religions, corporations, etc., all seek to exert greater control over their environment, which usually leads to a desire to control other organizations and those within them. However, these organizations experience the same negatives when exercising hard power as do individuals. An example is a nation state that uses its highly feared military to intervene but struggles to achieve its military objectives as easily as it envisioned (e.g., the US in Vietnam or the Soviet Union in Afghanistan). These nations' power declined by their exercise of hard power. Compare this to a nation exercising cultural influence (e.g., ancient China or Renaissance France). Their soft power influenced other nations to such an extent that French became literally the lingua franca of world diplomacy. The use of hard power can also directly diminish soft power. For example, at the onset of the Russian Revolution, the ideals of Communism had a lot of cachet among intellectuals in the US and Europe. However, by the time people understood Stalinism and its extreme oppression, Stalin had effectively destroyed the influence of Communism beyond the Iron Curtain.

Freedom

"If you love freedom for yourself, but not for others, then it is privilege you love" - unknown

The word "freedom" only appears in the US Constitution one time, and not in the original text. It is in the third article of the Bill of Rights, which states that Congress shall make no laws prohibiting the free exercise of religion, or "abridging the freedom of speech, or of the press; or the right of the people peaceably to assemble, and to petition the Government for a redress of grievances."

The Bill of Rights enumerates other rights (e.g., right to a trial by jury), but these freedoms of religion, press, assembly and petitions for redress are the only "freedoms" in the Constitution. Of course, there are many other references to freedom in US lore, such as "land of the free" in the National Anthem. So, what does the word "freedom" mean as envisioned by the founders of our nation? Looking up "freedom" in the dictionary, there are three primary definitions: 1) the power to act, think or speak without hindrance or restraint; 2) absence of subjugation by a foreign or despotic government; or 3) the state of not being imprisoned or enslaved.

I think it's clear that the Constitution does not refer to the third definition, as there are references to both imprisonment and slavery within the Constitution. So, it's likely that the founders were referring to the first two definitions. The American Revolution was a reaction to what was viewed in America as oppression of the American colonies by the government of Great Britain in the 18th century. There was a fundamental difference in perspective between the American colonists and the government in London as to the status of those living in the American colonies. The Americans viewed themselves as English citizens, with all the rights of English citizens. The English government viewed the Americas as a possession of England, not unlike other English colonies. The fundamental difference is that, in many other English colonies, the English colonial administration was ruling subject (i.e., conquered) peoples. The English government, and by extension, the English people, were amazingly ignorant of the people inhabiting the Americas. For example, not all Englishmen even realized that most of the American colonists were white-skinned and spoke English! The gap between the English government's perspective on the people inhabiting the American colonies and the way those colonists viewed themselves would prove to be so large as to be insurmountable. Given this background, as well as the contemporaneous writings of the time, it is clear that freedom from subjugation by a despotic (meaning cruel and oppressive) government was at the heart of what the framers of the Constitution had in mind.

What of the first definition? The freedom to act, think or speak without hindrance? We know that freedom of speech was considered, as it is specifically enumerated. One can only presume that if one is free to speak without constraint, one is also free to think without constraint. That leaves freedom to act without constraint. It is clear in the Constitution that the freedom to act is somewhat limited. Piracy, counterfeiting and treason are specifically listed as crimes within the Constitution itself. So, citizens are clearly not free to engage in these activities. But the Constitution also lists rights of citizens, such as freedom to practice one's chosen religion. So, presumably, any actions by one citizen to constrain another citizen's enumerated rights would be antithetical to the Bill of Rights.

The Constitution was the primary governing document for the newly created US government. It discusses the relationship between the federal government and the states and citizens of the newly formed country. Before the Constitution, there was only a loose confederation of states which had come together for the intent purpose of overthrowing English rule. Every power granted to the federal government came at the expense of state governments (and their citizens). So, those relationships were necessarily the focus of the document, rather than the relationships between citizens, which are primarily governed by state laws, even to this day. Therefore, the perspective of the Constitution, especially given the recent overthrow of despotic English rule and the suspicion the states had of granting excessive powers to the federal government, was to limit the powers of the federal government over its citizens. Many of the rights specifically addressed by the Bill of Rights were from perceived abuses of power by the British government (e.g., quartering soldiers in private homes). So, when referring to "freedom" in the context of the founding of the United States, I think it is clear that "freedom from tyranny" is the primary freedom being addressed.

These points seem to be self-evident, but some people have been talking about freedom in a different way. They seem to interpret "freedom" to mean something akin to the freedom to remake the nation in line with their beliefs. Examples would include the freedom to not only bear

61

arms but to assault people assumed to be a potential threat, or freedom not only to practice one's religion, but to impose one's religious beliefs upon others, or the freedom to utilize federal lands for personal enrichment. Of course, none of these examples are freedoms, but privileges. A privilege is a special right or advantage possessed by a person or a group of people. The exercise of privileges usually involves infringement upon the rights of others. If all had equal rights, it would not be possible to exercise privilege. While the Constitution explicitly acknowledges some privileges (the right to own slaves and the right of only males to vote being the most glaring examples), these exceptions prove the rule that the general philosophy of the Constitution is to expand the rights of citizens by limiting the role of government to enforce privileges. In fact, Article 12 of the Bill of Rights specifically states that any powers that are not specifically granted to the federal government are reserved for the states and their peoples.

Privilege unlawfully exercised has another meaning: injustice. And, as Martin Luther King said, "Injustice anywhere is a threat to justice everywhere." So, as we celebrate our freedoms in line with the ideals of the founders of our nation, it is important to always test these freedoms against the rights of others. That is truly the spirit upon which the nation was founded, and the Bill of Rights was adopted.

Love and Marriage

"Marriage is a wonderful institution. But who wants to live in an institution?" - Groucho Marx

The history of love and marriage has gone through many evolutions over time, and there are still very different expectations for these concepts depending on geography, culture, class status and other factors. Marriage started out as primarily an economic institution. It didn't represent the fulfillment of couples' desire to live with each other but rather the merger of families, both for the benefit of combining the families' economic strengths as well as the continuation of the family lines. Children were the only security most elderly people had, so marriage was also an institution for securing assistance, especially in old age. Eventually, the love component of marriage became more important (though not necessarily in all cultures) and the economic and child-bearing aspects receded in importance. Also, with women able to pursue their own careers, the reliance of women on men for economic security has also diminished. Finally, sexual liberation and the availability of birth control means that marriage is no longer the only acceptable context for sexual relations. This transition has become so complete in western society that the rate of marriage has steadily decreased. In 1970, the marriage rate in the US was over 76%. By 2020, the marriage rate stood at just over 30%. Conversely, the birth rate for children outside of marriage has increased from just 18% in 1980 to 40% in 2022. So, the very foundation for marriage seems to be on shaky ground.

However, when one analyzes the data in more granular detail, the irrelevance of marriage becomes less clear. The marriage rates for middle- and upper-class Americans is more than double that of poor Americans (56% vs. 26%). Similarly, while the rate of out-of-wedlock children among the poor is 64%, the rate of out-of-wedlock children for middle- and upper-income families is a mere 13%, lower than even the average rate in 1980. This poses the question as to whether poorer people are more likely to be single parents, or whether single parents are more likely to be poor. While the data does not give an entirely certain answer, the most likely answer is "both." That is because, whatever the original reasons for out-of-wedlock births, there can be no denying that the financial and time burdens of raising children are more difficult to absorb alone.

Turning next to love, this is a word that is burdened with many meanings in English. The definition of love in

English encompasses romantic love, familial love, love for friends and companions and even passion for favorite activities, foods, or items. It is obviously difficult to equate a love of dancing with a love for a parent. For this purpose, we will focus on love for a spouse, romantic partner, or life partner. Even narrowing the focus to these special people still leaves a great deal of complexity. Different psychologists enumerate various stages of this sort of love. However, they basically break down their stages into the early phases, characterized by infatuation, the thrill of discovery and blindness to the partner's faults and then into more long-term (companionate) phases, characterized by adjustment, compromise and commitment to the relationship.

For long-term relationships to be successful requires commitment, flexibility, work and luck. That is because not only does love evolve over time, but the people in the relationship also change. John Gottman, a professor of psychology at the University of Illinois (and later the University of Washington) has written extensively on marriage and long-term relationships and he developed the Gottman method for couples counseling. He claims to be able to predict whether a couple will stay together or divorce with 94% accuracy based upon a single counseling session. While having couples discuss a matter that they disagree about, Gottman-method practitioners observe the way in which a couple treats each other. Successful couples can discuss a disagreement while maintaining respect and without personalizing the argument. Unsuccessful couples will exhibit one or more of the "Four Horsemen of the Apocalypse" (criticism, contempt, defensiveness and stonewalling). Gottman has determined that couples in a broken relationship exhibit the same "fight or flight" stresses when around each other as experienced in other, stressful situations. Successful couples, by contrast, can exert a calming influence on each other.

So, are married people happier and more successful? And what about children? Are married couples happier if they have children, or not? Unfortunately, the data behind these questions offers no clear-cut answers. It would suggest that, in and of itself, choosing to be married or choosing to have children does not make people significantly more or less happy. As with many aspects of life, people disposed to happiness can find satisfaction in multiple circumstances, and people disposed to unhappiness can find reasons to be unhappy in many circumstances. It does seem that happier people are more likely to become married and more likely to find satisfaction in marriage, but divorce and death of a partner have a negative (but not necessarily permanent) impact on happiness.

My own conclusions, from a combination of personal experience, research and anecdotal conversations with friends and family would indicate the following. Life will be difficult at times and having a life partner you can count on can be very helpful. Also, learning to love and support someone can be a source of personal development and satisfaction. So, being in a positive, successful long-term relationship with a life partner may be the best possible circumstance for many people. However, being in a dysfunctional, abusive or stressful long-term relationship can be amongst the most difficult of circumstances. Said differently, it may be best to be with the right person, but better to be single than with the wrong person. So, like many things in life, the institution of marriage is neither inherently good nor bad, but it is what we make of it. I do think that any long-term relationship will go through periods of difficulty, when each partner's commitment to the relationship may be put to the test. Being in the legal and societal structure of marriage may be supportive during such times. However, the converse is that a bad marriage is more difficult to dissolve than a bad relationship.

Dad, Unsolicited

For myself, I cannot imagine my life without my wife. She is my life partner and my best friend. I also find each of my children to be great blessings in my life. However, I realize that my experience is not universal. Making yourself vulnerable also makes you exposed. I know many couples who have been through terribly painful divorces, and other couples who have experienced the deep loss of estranged or deceased children. But, to be truly known by someone, yet still loved, is liberating. Many poets and musicians have written far more eloquently about love and loss than I could ever attempt. Perhaps Tennyson expressed it best when he said "'Tis better to have loved and lost, than never to have loved at all."

As for marriage, if it is to survive as an institution, it will need to continue to evolve from its original purposes to adapt to a modern world. That said, I hope it can survive as I believe the societal support and recognition marriage offers to long-term relationships can be beneficial to all parties.

Foxes and Hedgehogs

"Our comforting conviction that the world makes sense rests on a secure foundation: our almost unlimited ability to ignore our ignorance." - Daniel Kahneman

In the 7th century BC, Archilochus, the Greek poet, wrote: "A fox knows many things, but a hedgehog knows one big thing" Since that time, poets, philosophers and psychologists have argued about whether it is better to be a fox or a hedgehog. A "Hedgehog" has one overarching construct for the universe in which everything fits (e.g., a religion or a political philosophy). A "Fox" draws from many different, often conflicting, sources in attempting to understand the universe. A Hedgehog is more likely to try to figure out how new information fits into and supports their view of the universe, while a Fox is more likely to adjust their thinking in the light of new information. Isaiah Berlin defined and rekindled this debate within his 1953 book, The Hedgehog and the Fox, in which he attempted to place famous writers and thinkers throughout history into either category.

Being a hedgehog is tempting. It is easier, and somehow more comfortable, to try to fit the world into a nice, consistent package; to live in a world with a purpose and structure. This provides us with hope that we can, in fact, understand the universe and our place in it. Further, once we understand it, we can live by the rules of that universe, and therefore have some control over our own lives. If you desire to be a famous writer, philosopher or influencer, you would be better served to be a hedgehog. Your ability to persuade others that you understand the secrets of the universe will motivate them to read and follow you. This ability will substantially increase if there is a model that you have created that you can explain to them which seems to answer all of life's questions. It will fit the human desire to comprehend nature and its laws. That is why many famous writers, pundits and experts are hedgehogs. One need only review the "experts" on social media to find a vast array of people attempting to fit everything they have experienced into a nice, tidy explanation. One could even argue that this very collection of essays is much the same. The alternative view (the Fox), that the world is random and defies complete understanding, is inherently terrifying for many people (plus it will not gain you many followers on social media). The Fox's view of the universe is constantly shifting, evolving and changing. It is inherently less satisfying to never be sure that you have things figured out. To the Fox, understanding consists of layers: feeling that you understand an aspect of the world, but then, as you learn more, realizing that there are still things you don't fully understand. It is to exist in, and be comfortable with, a constant state of uncertainty.

However, in his book Expert Political Judgment, University of Pennsylvania professor of political psychology Philip Tetlock summarized research that showed that, while most pundits and experts were hedgehogs, they were very poor at forecasting. The Foxes had much better results because they used more data points and were more open to challenging their conclusions.

We have a strong evolutionary bias towards believing we have made correct conclusions. An animal which cannot decide between fight or flight is paralyzed and will not survive. Deciding has certain advantages. It is a bias towards action, away from passivity. Most of the time, deciding on some course of action is far better than remaining passively frozen in indecision. However, we must recognize that feeling we are "right" is an emotion, not the result of a logical process. Conviction that we are right *feels* comfortable. Fitting our experiences into a coherent worldview is also comfortable. We must understand that this "comfortable" feeling is unrelated to whether we are, in fact, correct.

In fact, this feeling of comfort typically creates resistance to other data and perspectives that suggest we may be wrong. We force facts into our hedgehog's worldview rather than use additional data to challenge our assumptions. The stronger our convictions, the more resistant we are to contrary information. This is why William Brinkley advised "Always consider the possibility that you may be wrong. Especially when you are absolutely certain you are right."

So, how to resolve the dichotomy between needing to make conclusions to avoid paralysis and wanting to arrive at correct decisions? The answer is movement with course corrections. In the same way that one starts on a long journey, but often needs to alter course because of new information along the way (construction, weather, wrong turns, etc.), one has to be willing to begin a course of action, but also be open to course-correct along the way. This means listening with an open mindset.

Most of the time, we listen to "win" or to "fix". Listening to win means preparing to negate the other person's observations. This can be done with the best of intentions. For example, we can try to reassure someone (e.g., "I look fat!" "No, you look great!") Listening to fix means preparing to solve the other person's issues with solutions.

73

While both responses can be useful in the right situations, they both begin with the premise that we are right. Sometimes people need to "win" because being right is wrapped up into their self-identity, which is why Wallace Sayre famously quipped "Academic politics are so vicious precisely because the stakes are so small."

Open minded listening, by contrast, is listening to learn information we may not have already. It involves asking questions, paraphrasing what you think you've already heard back to the person, and generally trying to more fully understand their perspective. It is less comfortable and takes more effort, which is why most people do it rarely. But it can be worth it. If you are wrong, you may learn things that help you form better conclusions. If you are right, it can be much more persuasive as the other person is along for the journey and feels heard. And most times we will be partially right (or wrong) and listening with an open mind allows us to continue on our own journey but make the more minor changes that help us arrive at our desired outcomes.

My beliefs have evolved greatly over the course of my life. Many of the things I once accepted as true I have come to believe are not. One of the most fundamental, and disturbing, changes I have experienced is that I no longer believe that there is any systematic explanation of the universe where it will "all make sense." Unfortunately for us, the universe either defies any explanation, or such an explanation is far too complicated for us to understand. While to some that can be a depressing idea, to me this signifies our own responsibility for the choices we make in our lives. There is no set of "rules" that we can just follow. Instead, we must be constantly evolving our actions and beliefs to fit our current circumstances. And, while our choices cannot ensure our success or happiness, they can ensure that we have lived our very best possible life, subject to the whims of fortune and chance.

Building a Family

"All happy families are alike; each unhappy family is unhappy in its own way." - Leo Tolstoy, <u>Anna Karenina</u>

This is my favorite quote about families, because I think it so succinctly describes the challenge of a happy family. I often picture a narrow plank over a swamp - where a step to either side results in immersion into the swamp. We all know probably many more unhappy than happy families. So many different elements need to come together to create a happy family, many outside the control of any individual member and some also beyond the control of all the members. So, while I will, somewhat hesitantly, offer some of my own thoughts on this topic, I do so both with a sense of humility in that I hardly consider myself the architect of my seemingly happy family and gratitude in that I realize how lucky I am. Finally, a family is a dynamic thing. One day's happy (or unhappy) family can shift course suddenly due to external or internal pressures. Even excluding external factors people change over time. Certainly, children change dramatically over time, but even most adults continue to grow and evolve their views over time. This means that families must be able to continually adapt to new circumstances and "happiness", once achieved, may only be momentary.

With those caveats behind me, I will offer some thoughts. Unsurprisingly, a happy family will begin with a happy marriage. I cannot imagine how a family functions successfully with a couple that are dissatisfied with their choice in a partner. One of the most ridiculous comments one sometimes hears is "We had a baby to save our marriage." While a birth may have contributed to a couple staying together out of a shared sense of obligation, it seems very unlikely to me that a baby can make an unhappy couple happy. That is because a baby, as much as they may be loved by her parents, is undoubtedly a source of additional stress upon a marriage. The lack of sleep, stress over the health of the baby, additional financial burdens, decrease in personal time: these are all stresses upon a couple and, if they are already on rocky ground, the addition of a baby will only make things worse.

It is not my intention in this essay to go into depth about the elements of a successful marriage. I do try to address some aspects of marriage in another essay. However, I do think that a theme for a successful marriage and a happy family is a willingness to forgo dominance. It's a natural human impulse to want to dominate others. We see this even in other primates, which almost always feature a strict social hierarchy. However, for one person to give into their desire to dominate within the context of a family requires the other family members to accede to that dominance, or to resist. The latter will make for an unstable family. The former will likely lead to resentment over the long term. Forgoing dominance does not mean forgoing leadership. Dominance is forcing one's will upon another. Leadership is about guiding a group towards a common goal. Leadership is an action, not a position. Leadership enhances trust within the group. Dominance reduces trust. Leadership guides and develops others. Dominance stunts the development of the rest of the members of the family.

Of course, parents do need to take a dominant position with small children. A child is not prepared at birth to assume sole responsibility for their own life. This is obvious. However, I think one of the main philosophical differences in raising children among parents is the balance between goals in raising children: independence vs. safety.

Of course, both goals are important, and the first responsibility of any parent is to ensure the safety of children until they can begin to look after themselves; a gradual process. I would also speculate that most parents do not systematically map out these goals and decide in a conscious way how they will prioritize them. And, in two-parent families, there may be a large divergence in how each parent prioritizes these goals. Certainly, my wife leaned more towards the safety side while I pushed more for independence. Hopefully, these two viewpoints yielded an appropriate balance. Regardless of whether the result of conscious choices or not, how parents approach these two fundamental objectives in raising children will have a profound effect on both the development of children and on the success of the family dynamic.

In earlier times, family resources could be quite limited. Simply ensuring enough food for the family could be a struggle. In such an environment, children's need to develop independent survival skills was accelerated. There was a somewhat Darwinian effect in that children who could not quickly develop survival skills could be subject to calamity. Diseases also impacted child safety, such that as late as the 18th century, between 40-50% of European-born children died before their 15th birthday. This staggering mortality rate for children devastated many families and shaped societies in profound ways. Fortunately, child mortality dropped precipitously throughout the 19th and 20th centuries such that, by 1950 in the US, less than 4% of children died before they were 5 years old.

As living standards increased, and child mortality decreased, family sizes also tended to shrink. Thus, each child was arguably "more valuable" to their parents as parents would presumably be more devastated by the loss of their only child than of one child in 15. This, combined with increasing resources, tipped the scales towards safety over independence, as families could concentrate more resources in preserving the safety of each child.

Another major factor in parenting has been the revolution in communications. Until the mid-1990s, once a child left their home, they were difficult to contact. Teens congregated at malls and restaurants, effectively out of the reach of their parents. Once they left for college, contact between parents and their children was very limited and infrequent. As a result, these adolescents were often forced to solve problems for themselves, without input from their parents. With the widespread use of cell phones beginning in the 1990s, parents could always be in reach of their children, resulting in terms like "helicopter parents" (always hovering) and "bulldozer parents" (removing all obstacles before their children). It's also beyond the scope of this essay to address increasing levels of mental and emotional anxiety in young people, but I believe one of the factors may be the lowered confidence possessed by children who are seldom given the opportunity to make decisions by themselves.

In some ways, this additional time spent between parents and children has clear benefits in terms of closer relations between parents and children. However, it can also delay the transition from a parent-child relationship to a parent-adult relationship. In fact, psychologists have been writing about a delayed entrance to adulthood by young people today compared to earlier generations. This is also too complex and multi-faceted an issue to deal with here, but I believe parents are often largely to blame in that, intentionally or not, they may seek to keep their children dependent on them (emotionally or financially) as a means of securing their place in their children's lives. It is also a way for parents to maintain a certain level of control over their children's choices (of career, romantic partner, living location, etc.). This allows the parents, to some degree, to justify their own life choices by influencing their children to make very similar choices. This is somewhat counterintuitive as often the parents are unhappy with their choices yet seem determined to cause their children to follow these choices, nonetheless. This generally stunts and even destroys the relationship the parents are working so feverishly to preserve, because children inevitably seek to make their own choices as they mature, creating a conflict between parent and child. As the now adult child seeks to establish their independence, some parents grow ever more desperate to maintain control, via financial incentives or expressed criticisms of their children's choices, which can drive the children even further away from these parents, ultimately creating estrangement. Even when the parents succeed in maintaining their control, the child grows resentful of their dependence and will ultimately blame their parents for their failure to establish their own, independent lives. So, the parents' desire for control creates a lose-lose situation of resentment, immaturity and possibly codependence.

Developmental milestones are coded into our genetics and cannot be denied without negative consequences. Just as a baby is compelled to begin to walk, an adolescent is compelled to break away from their parents. If the parents try too long to maintain control over the adolescent, they set up a conflict that cannot be avoided. Better for the parents to have the objective of preparing their children to be independent adults, willing and able to make their own decisions with confidence vs. trying to maintain dependence and thereby control. In my opinion, this starts early by giving children responsibilities (e.g., doing their own chores), opportunities to succeed or fail and suffering the consequences of poor choices, within the context of safety. Allowing children to overcome bad choices and failures is what gives them the confidence and resilience to make their own choices and overcome adversity. The "bulldozer" parent style creates children that do not feel confident in their own abilities and choices.

This requires a difficult transition on the part of parents and is one of the hardest adjustments to the relationship for parents to recognize and execute successfully. The parent must work with their child to transition from a controlling, safety-oriented parent-child relationship to a supportive counselor. The parent needs to resist constantly substituting their opinions for their child's and refrain from the temptation of using their often-greater resources to influence their children's choices. By allowing their adult children to take control of their own lives, but remaining engaged and supportive, parents can manage the necessary transition in the relationship, providing guidance and support, but only when asked.

Adult children have their own role to play in a successful transition. It is almost impossible to grow up completely free of the childhood baggage from the family's dynamic, even after leaving home. This means that children may react to parental advice as criticism, or parental offers of help as evidence of a lack of confidence. Finally, as parents reach their old-age, the usual parent-child relationship often reverses, with the child needing to oversee the decisions of the parent. Hopefully, love, empathy and trust can smooth over the inevitable emotions between family members and maintain positive parent-child bonds through the several transitions that will occur in these critical relationships as both go through their future life stages.

Can Men and Women Be Friends?

Harry: Because no man can be friends with a woman that he finds attractive. He always wants to have sex with her.

Sally: So, you're saying that a man *can* be friends with a woman he finds unattractive?

Harry: No, you pretty much want to nail 'em too.

Sally: What if *they* don't want to have sex with *you?*

Harry: Doesn't matter because the sex thing is already out there so the friendship is ultimately doomed and that is the end of the story.

Sally: Well, I guess we're not going to be friends then.

Harry: Guess not.

Sally: That's too bad. You were the only person that I knew in New York.

Nora Ephron, "When Harry Met Sally"

The movie "When Harry Met Sally" came out in 1989 and I was just a few years out of college. In some ways, the timing of this question being raised in the movie was well-matched with my stage of life. I had graduated college three years ago, had just gotten married, yet had several women friends, both holdovers from college and people I had met at work. While I could understand Harry's (played

by Billy Crystal) point of view, I rejected it. I still do. However, it is a reasonable question because some men and
some women are not successful at being friends (either they
do not view each other as potential friends or their friendship evolves (devolves?) into something romantic). It's also
true that it may be easier for men and women to be friends
at some stages of life than others. So, I have given some
thought to the barriers between men and women generally,
and why their relationships can be more challenging than
same-sex relationships. My observations are both from ob-
serving others and my own interactions and my perspective
is male and heterosexual.

First, the relationships between men and women
change over time largely because of the maturity (or lack
thereof) of the participants. Even as children, relationships
between boys and girls, which do not yet have a romantic
dimension, are still shaped by society. Other children and
even adults may tease about these relationships and the children themselves may play-act gender roles they observe in
adults. Then, as these children enter puberty, they begin to
view the opposite sex with some potent mix of desire and
fear which can make interactions awkward and rare. In high
school and college, most people are not usually in serious
relationships with the opposite sex, which means that, when

they do interact, they usually are evaluating the other person as a potential romantic interest, or maybe a backup romantic interest if their current pursuit is unsuccessful.

Over time, most men and women develop the ability to view each other as fellow human beings more than potential mates, which opens the door to the possibility of friendship. But this process is not a consistent or linear one. First, some men never move beyond their desire to evaluate every woman as a potential mate, even when such relationships would be inappropriate due to age or power differences. This attitude, which in extreme cases can become predatory, is a result of arrested development on the part of the man. It may be due to the man's inability to form successful, healthy romantic relationships with women, which causes him to continually be searching for a woman with whom to develop such a relationship. But this is not always the case. It may be as simple as a man lacking the emotional maturity to realize that not all his desires need to be gratified, a type of privileged thinking. Either way, it is likely rooted in a lack of empathy, both for the object of his desire as well as the impact his behavior has on others (e.g., his family, his organization, and his own reputation). Women will criticize this behavior as selfish, privileged and predatory (all of which is true), but it also is a weakness. Many is the man who has undone his family, his career, his standing and even his freedom in pursuit of his desires.

Of course, women can also be guilty of these sorts of attitudes, but it seems less common. It may be as simple as less women have the power to pursue this sort of predatory behavior. However, there are also women whose self-esteem rests to some degree on their perceived attractiveness to men. This may cause them to approach men in a more flirtatious manner, which may preclude them viewing each other as potential platonic friends.

Another factor in whether men and women can be friends is whether each party is already in a committed romantic relationship. There is some dialogue in "When Harry Met Sally" that attempts to address this situation:

Harry: Would you like to have dinner? ...Just friends.
Sally: I thought you didn't believe men and women could be friends.
Harry: When did I say that?
Sally: On the ride to New York.
Harry: No, no, no, no, I never said that... Yes, that's right, they can't be friends...unless both of them are involved with other people. Then they can. This is an amendment to the

earlier rule. If the two people are in relationships, the pressure of possible involvement is lifted. That doesn't work either. Because what happens then is the person you're involved with can't understand why you need to be friends with the person you're just friends with, like it means something is missing from the relationship and you wanted to go outside to get it. Then when you say, 'No, no, no, no, it's not true, nothing is missing from the relationship,' the person you're involved with then accuses you of being secretly attracted to the person you're just friends with, which you probably are - I mean, come on, who the hell are we kidding, let's face it - which brings us back to the earlier rule before the amendment, which is men and women can't be friends. So where does it leave us?

Sally: Goodbye Harry.

Of course, "When Harry Met Sally" is intended as comedy, but there is an underlying truth in this exchange. When a man and woman are friends, and there is not "the pressure of possible involvement" their partners may still view the "friend" as a potential threat to the relationship. Even when the intentions of both friends may be innocent, the difficulties of explaining this relationship to their romantic partner may outweigh the benefit of maintaining it. This explains why couples usually socialize with other couples.

This can create difficulties for singles whose friends are married because they don't fit easily into their previously single friend's new social dynamic. I would also note that, in my observation, while a marriage may be viewed as a sacred commitment by the married person, a single, opposite sex acquaintance may not view their acquaintance's marriage as seriously. They may even feel that fidelity in a marriage is solely between the married parties, and that they bear no responsibility in that matter. So, a close, platonic relationship between men and women is more likely to succeed when both are in committed romantic relationships rather than just one party.

Of course, even when both parties are married, opposite-sex friends may inadvertently develop romantic feelings for the other. However, as discussed elsewhere, one should not always act on their feelings, which are being driven by emotions developed through evolution and not necessarily aligned with a person's long-term happiness. By maintaining the platonic nature of the relationship, these romantic feelings will likely fade over time. There is another advantage to being disciplined in this way. An affair will need to be resolved in some way - either through ending the affair or ending the existing committed relationship (e.g., marriage). If both relationships are valuable, the only way to maintain these relationships over the long-term is to avoid the sort of betrayals that will inevitably lead to the dissolution of one or both. Few people can maintain activities that they view as "wrong" over a long-term.

So, the answer to the question of "Can men and women be friends?" is "Yes, of course they can." However, these relationships require a level of maturity and discipline that not all people will be capable of at all points in their lives. Some people may never be capable of these relationships, but that does not mean that they cannot be valuable and enriching relationships for those that are.

Granfalloons

"Granfalloon is a proud and meaningless collection of human beings" - Kurt Vonnegut

Granfalloon is the idea that people share something in common, even though they otherwise don't know each other. A synonym for Granfalloon could be "tribe". Most of our brains are devoted to keeping track of social relationships, not just direct relationships to ourselves, but relationships between people. Studies show that the ideal grouping for humans is between 80-100 people. You can know that many people and you can also keep track of generally how they exist in relation to each other. One of the theories as to why homo sapiens was more successful than Neanderthals, was that the groupings of homo sapiens were larger, and they were thus able to push Neanderthal groups outside of preferred hunting grounds.

Another aspect of tribes is that they are hostile to non-members. In a world of limited resources, it is natural that a tribe would need to defend its territory, and thus the associated resources, from intruders. We see this same behavior in the wild with chimpanzees and other primates.

However, this behavior, so well suited for the plains of Africa, can cause problems in a modern, globe-spanning society.

At their best, granfalloons can offer a way for strangers to find common ground and initiate a relationship. For example, you notice another person wearing the team colors for your school or the name of your favorite music group and it allows one to start a conversation. The danger of these tenuous relationships ensues when one over-identifies with what is essentially a meaningless connection and it causes a person to view with suspicion, or even hostility, a person of another group. This is occurring now in the US with political parties. In recent polls some party members viewed fellow Americans of a different party as more dangerous to the country than governments of clearly hostile powers. Granfalloons can also cause people to make assumptions about the other person, positive or negative, which are unwarranted. This can cause misplaced trust, as commonly evidenced by fraud committed within religious groups because a member of one's religion is viewed as trustworthy without any further information.

Nowhere is this misplaced identification potentially more damaging than with regards to race. To begin with, race is an artificial construct, and most people are a mixture of ethnicities, so it's difficult sometimes to even identify a person's race or understand what it means. However, some people persist in making assumptions about others based upon a quick assessment of the other's race. And even more perplexing are the bigoted calls for the "preservation of the white race" as if there was such a thing as the white race, and as if such a racial identity carried any meaning whatsoever.

Race, like all granfalloons, is a social construct, not a biological one. Before the 1500s, the term "race" was hardly used. When it was used, it denoted groups of people with kinship. At that time, people were categorized more by their religious beliefs (pagan, Jew, Catholic, Protestant, Muslim, etc.) than their physical features. Wars were fought and people were still slaughtered, but it was because of their religious beliefs vs. their skin color. The concept of race as we know it today was developed in conjunction with the European Enlightenment of the 17th century. Without religion to categorize people, philosophers needed a new basis to group peoples. The Enlightenment embraced the idea of "natural laws" that governed the world and human society. Unfortunately, these ideas were co-opted by Europeans as justification for colonization and race-based slavery. The "white" race, which had not really existed as a concept previously, and became a stand-in for Europeans, was considered to be inherently smarter, more capable and more civilized than other races. Therefore, it was only natural that the white race dominates the people and territory of other, lesser races. This fits nicely into European imperialism and the competition between European nations to claim territories around the globe. These justifications were most poetically summarized in Rudyard Kipling's "The White Man's Burden" poem, written to encourage American annexation of the Philippines in the 19th century.

Slavery has existed for most of human society, but it was not originally race-based. Typically, slaves came from conquered peoples. Many ancient societies depended on slaves to make their economies function. Part of the Roman Empire's drive for ever more conquests was their need to replenish the slaves upon which their economy depended. Romans even used Greek slaves as teachers, administrators and civil servants, so there was not a concept that slaves were necessarily less intelligent (just less fortunate). However, as Europeans colonized the Americas and developed plantations for growing sugar, coffee and other crops, the need for low cost but hardy workers increased. European diseases and overwork had killed off much of the native populations of the Americas. African slaves became the solution to both plantation owners' need for workers who could survive the very harsh conditions of tropical plantations, and merchants' need to fill ships on both the westbound (slaves) and east-bound (rum, sugar, coffee, etc.) trans-Atlantic passages. Africans alleged racial inferiority became the justification for such a blatantly inhumane system. As the North American colonies were developed and cotton became the major crop of the American south, the same justifications were used to import slaves to North America.

Even after slavery was abolished in the United States after the Civil War, the concept of racial disparity was so embedded in American society by that point that it persisted. Politicians found racial bigotry and ideas of racial purity fertile ground on which to plant seeds of division between people to be exploited for votes.

As noted above, granfalloons allow people to assume connections with others which may not actually exist. Race-based granfalloons allow some people (usually poor whites) to assume that they merit a higher status in society. This makes it difficult for those who feel they benefit (or should benefit) to give up on the racial construct. However, the sad truth is that these expected race-based entitlements are seldom worth much. The wealthy and powerful are happy to utilize racial hierarchies to maintain their own power, but the benefits to the poor are mostly illusory. That's why Lyndon Johnson famously stated, ""If you can convince the lowest white man he's better than the best colored man, he won't notice you're picking his pocket. Hell, give him somebody to look down on, and he'll empty his pockets for you."

Granfalloons can be harmless fun and can open people to connections they might not otherwise initiate. But granfalloons that are based on race, or nationalism, are often exploited by politicians and autocrats as a way of maintaining power. Not to mention that these divisions are very often a source of great injustice. Therefore, the sooner we can move beyond assumptions about each other and judge others solely by the "content of their character" as Martin Luther King dreamed, the better off we will all be.

Solving the World's Problems

Rabbi: "Only a fool thinks he can solve the world's problems"

Man: "Yeah, but you gotta try, don't ya?"

Fargo, Season 2

One of the fundamental questions of life is how to respond to the needs of others. Jesus uses the parable of the Good Samaritan to explain that everyone is our "neighbor" and thus deserving of our love and assistance. However, the needs of the world are clearly overwhelming for any one individual, and it would be a fool who thinks he can solve the world's problems. So, what then is the appropriate response?

We see this play out in society all the time: from students protesting the foreign policies of the government on their campuses to people dressed as Santas ringing their bells for the Salvation Army during the holidays. Perhaps the students have set their ambitions too high, as the likelihood that campus protests will alter government policies may be low. But does that give us permission to pass by the Santas at Christmas? How to respond on the spectrum of sacrifice between the poles of Mother Theresa and Ebenezer Scrooge (pre-spirits visitation)?

The answer for each person ultimately must be an individual choice, but I will offer the perspective once heard in a sermon: "What if every job was done by a Christian?" In other words, without the religious element, what if every person treated each other with love, respect and empathy in their daily interactions? I don't believe that most of us are capable of being a saint, but we likely are capable of endeavoring to respect and care for people who cross our paths. This alone is enough of a challenge for most of us. In Matthew 5:46-47 Jesus notes that even tax collectors (i.e., sinners) love those who love them, and even pagans greet their own families. So, the challenge for us is to treat even those whom we do not like, or do not know, with compassion.

This philosophy has selfish benefits as well as altruistic ones. Studies have shown that the most lasting path to individual happiness is to engage in acts of kindness (pro-social behaviors in the terminology of psychologists). The feeling that we are contributing to justice, compassion and charity makes us feel better about ourselves and thus makes us happier. Of course, this must be balanced by also taking care of our own needs. If we are destitute or depressed, we are unlikely to have much of a positive impact on the world around us. So, striking that balance between caring for our own needs without losing sight of how we can also care for others is the key to a sustainable level of happiness as well as a sustainable positive impact on the world.

Death

"Death awaits you all with nasty, big, pointy teeth!" - "Monty Python and the Holy Grail"

This is my favorite quote about death, because it is simultaneously true, silly, scary and profound. Probably nothing so inevitable is also simultaneously so ignored. We are literally born to die, but that truth is too paralyzing for most people to contemplate, so they simply proceed with their lives as if they will live forever. In fact, within "Monty Python and the Holy Grail," the very next line by King Arthur after receiving this warning is: "What an eccentric performance!" But, despite their denial, several of Arthur's knights are killed in the very next scene. While denying death is preferable to shrinking in fear, it also comes with some distinct disadvantages.

Our mortality, when we do contemplate it, can seem unfair. Delmore Schwartz in his famous poem "Calmly We Walk Through This April's Day" warns us repeatedly that "time is the fire in which we burn." Human literature has dealt many times with the desire for immortality, going as far back as the "Epic of Gilgamesh" dating to at least 2100 BC. Time is the one thing that we can never

101

get more of and the resource that we are most likely to over-estimate.

However, our limited time can also be a benefit. One can argue that much of our motivation to "make something of our lives" comes from the knowledge that our time to achieve anything is limited. As a child, I read a story about a race of immortals that just sat around. They were too afraid of accidental death to leave their homes and too confident in their unlimited time to be motivated to do anything today.

Another aspect of our limited time is the importance of nurturing and preserving our relationships. If we can live beyond our mortal lives, it is through the impact our lives had on those we love. It is also important to recognize that any interaction we have with someone could be our last and thus we should always take full advantage. When I was in my 30s, I visited my parents' house. The morning I was to leave, my father had an early morning golf game so we said our goodbyes the night before. That morning, I awoke early enough to see my father just exiting the house to catch a ride to his golf game. He did not notice me, and I contemplated calling out to him, but decided to leave him to catch his ride. It is the last time I ever laid eyes on him. For the past 25 years, this has been a constant reminder to me to make the most of every interaction.

My father's early death at 63 from a heart attack was a shock, but it also brought home to me the finite nature of our lives. I find that, in ignoring death because it is assumed to be "depressing," people also ignore the vital lesson that each of our days is important. Many people act as though their time is infinite because they are not comfortable pondering the truth. I find that many people continue working well past their financial needs, because they think the extra money from a few extra years of work is more important than the time they are sacrificing. Or maybe it is just that they do not feel the need to adjust their lives to retirement because it will be a difficult transition, and they can always do it "later."

But just as some people will live to 100, some will die relatively young. We have no idea how much time has been allotted to us, so we should act as if our time is perhaps more limited than it is. That means to take on those bucket list items while we have our health and our mental faculties. It means we should prioritize resolving estrangements with our family members. It means we should not waste time in passive activities but get out and make the most of each day.

Carpe Diem is not just an admonition; it is a warning by a long-dead Roman poet (Horace) who is telling us to be wise stewards of our most precious resource.

Final Thoughts

Ah, love, let us be true

To one another! for the world, which seems

To lie before us like a land of dreams,

So various, so beautiful, so new,

Hath really neither joy, nor love, nor light,

Nor certitude, nor peace, nor help for pain;

And we are here as on a darkling plain

Swept with confused alarms of struggle and flight,

Where ignorant armies clash by night.

- Matthew Arnold, "Dover Beach"

I was first introduced to "Dover Beach" by Leonard Bernstein as a teenager when watching one of his televised Young People's Concerts. In these programs, Bernstein would not only conduct but give brief lectures about the musical and creative backgrounds to the orchestral pieces. I don't recall which piece he conducted after introducing this last stanza of "Dover Beach", but I do recall the profound effect these lines had on me, now over forty years ago. This poem means so much to me that I have carried it in my work backpack for over thirty years so that I could refer to it.

105

Many people find the perspective of this poem depressing. People also find the idea of their own mortality depressing, something they desperately try to avoid thinking about. There is no doubt that life can be difficult at times and the world, which we enter with naive hopefulness, often disappoints us. I have observed many young people start out their careers with a generous optimism about their new life, only to learn that all human institutions, even those that purport to do good, are inherently flawed. Over time, they realize that they must become somewhat hardened to push through the inevitable difficulties and disappointments.

Many people act in selfish and even cruel ways. I believe that some do not really try to rise above their most base, animalistic impulses. But some do! For every cruel impulse, there is also kindness. For every destructive act, there have been creations of unimaginable beauty! It is up to each of us to try to become the very best version of ourselves.

Matthew Arnold wrote this poem on his honeymoon, a time of hopefulness. To me, the most important sentence is the first one. Yes, the world can be a dark place at times, but we can still be true! True to ourselves, true to our values, and true to one another. And our lives, while finite, do exist. Various people have calculated the odds of each of our individual existences as basically zero (one in 400 trillion). Each of our existences is essentially a miracle. The unlikeliness of our existence and the shortness of our lives relative to the scale of cosmic time means each moment is an unimaginable gift. And, although we ourselves may not exist forever among the living on earth, our impacts on others will reverberate for many years after we are gone. Just as we are the sum of all that came before us, we will add to that which comes after us. To quote Walt Whitman, "I am large, I contain multitudes." ("Song of Myself"). I believe we are meant to experience our lives as precious gifts, and to make the most of them, by being true. We have that opportunity. If we seize upon that opportunity, then we will have earned our rest.

"A man must fill his life with meaning, meaning is not automatically given to life. It is hard work to fill one's life with meaning...A life filled with meaning is worthy of rest. I want to be worthy of rest" - Chaim Potok

Acknowledgments

Over the course of my lifetime, I have tried to be observant and thoughtful. I have always been fascinated with why people behave the way that they do and tried to be thoughtful in making my own life decisions. The people that know me will agree that I have a lot of theories and opinions about why things are the way they are, and how we should respond. The untimely death of my father and dementia of my mother-in-law made me realize that all that we learn throughout our lives can be lost rather suddenly. This motivated me to write down some of these theories about life while I still had the capacity to do so. Not because I consider myself the wisest of people, but because I consider myself wiser now than in my youth, and it seems a shame for all that cumulative understanding to just be lost. I have joked with others that I wanted to provide my children with my thinking so that they can continue to ignore my advice even after I'm gone.

This is my first book, and I have learned a lot more than I expected through this process. Perhaps the biggest lesson is my even higher respect for authors who write from their own life experience. The more vulnerability an author exhibits, the more interesting the work. But such honesty is not easy. It impacts the image one may have cultivated for oneself as well as potentially impacting the feelings of those around you. I really admire those who can examine themselves with an objective eye, then report on their own mistakes to the outside world. I also have learned that writing a manuscript is only the first step in self-publishing a book. There are many other steps that take a great deal of time and are not inconsiderable in the overall effort. Nevertheless, the options for self-publishing available today allow someone like me to publish a small print run book that otherwise would never see the light of day.

I would like to thank Helen Raymaker, Sarah Fitch and Sarah Lindsey for reading some early drafts of this book and providing their comments. I would also like to thank my son, Luke Raymaker, for designing the cover. Finally, I thank anyone reading this for indulging me.

Guy Raymaker
Henderson, Nevada

About the Author

Guy Raymaker has nearly 40 years' experience as a licensed certified public accountant. He spent his entire career working for one of the world's largest public accounting and consultancy firms. He spent the last 10 years of his career in risk management, retiring as the firm's Deputy Chief Risk Officer where he designed organizations, systems and processes to help the firm better manage risk. Guy practiced in various offices including San Francisco, San Jose, Seattle, Chicago, New York and Tokyo, Japan.

Guy is a member of the American Institute of Certified Public Accountants and a past member of the Board of Directors of the Interfaith Food Pantry of Morris County, the San Jose Symphony and the American Model United Nations, which he co-founded. He has served as the treasurer of three churches. He currently resides in Henderson, NV with his wife and is the father to three adult children who work in the music, health and tech industries.